RIVER MONSTERS

ARAPAIMAS

BY JOANNE MATTERN

EPIC

Bellwether Media • Minneapolis, MN

EPIC

EPIC BOOKS are no ordinary books. They burst with intense action, high-speed heroics, and shadows of the unknown. Are you ready for an Epic adventure?

This edition first published in 2024 by Bellwether Media, Inc.

No part of this publication may be reproduced in whole or in part without written permission of the publisher. For information regarding permission, write to Bellwether Media, Inc., Attention: Permissions Department, 6012 Blue Circle Drive, Minnetonka, MN 55343.

Library of Congress Cataloging-in-Publication Data

LC record for Arapaimas available at: https://lccn.loc.gov/2023039879

Text copyright © 2024 by Bellwether Media, Inc. EPIC and associated logos are trademarks and/or registered trademarks of Bellwether Media, Inc.

Editor: Elizabeth Neuenfeldt   Designer: Josh Brink

Printed in the United States of America, North Mankato, MN.

TABLE OF CONTENTS

GIANT HUNTERS	4
BIG BODIES	6
FINDING FOOD	12
ARAPAIMAS IN TROUBLE	18
GLOSSARY	22
TO LEARN MORE	23
INDEX	24

GIANT HUNTERS

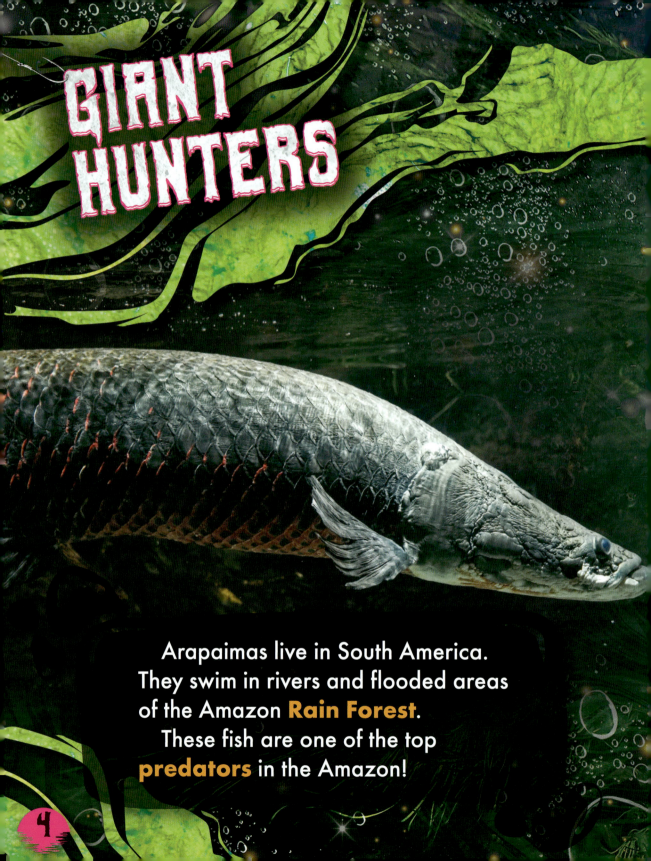

Arapaimas live in South America. They swim in rivers and flooded areas of the Amazon **Rain Forest**. These fish are one of the top **predators** in the Amazon!

MANY NAMES

Arapaimas have many names! In Brazil, they are called *pirarucu*. In Peru, people call them *paiche*.

ARAPAIMA RANGE

RANGE = ▭

BIG BODIES

Arapaimas are huge fish. They are among the largest **freshwater** fish in the world!

These fish can grow up to 15 feet (4.6 meters) long. They can weigh up to 440 pounds (200 kilograms)!

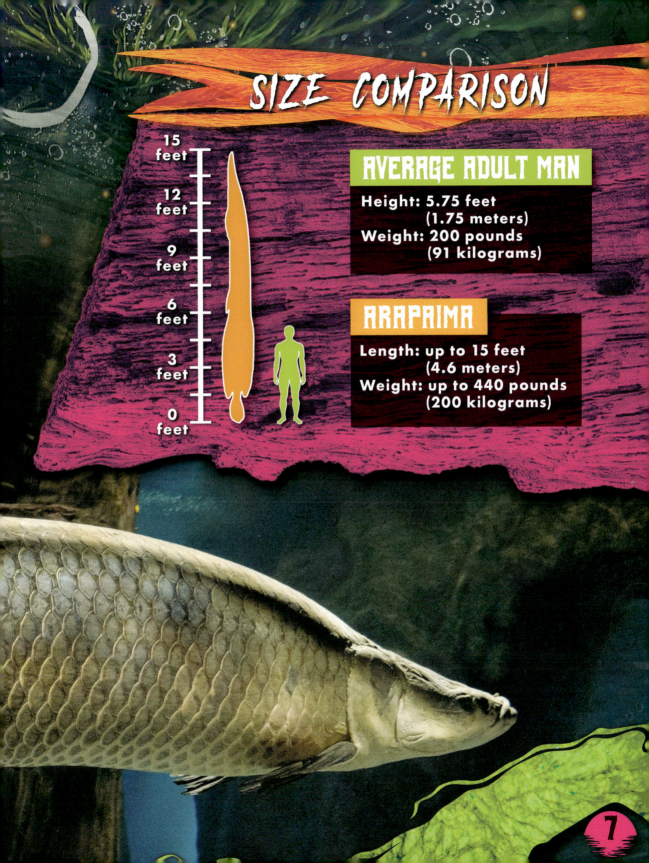

SIZE COMPARISON

AVERAGE ADULT MAN
Height: 5.75 feet
(1.75 meters)
Weight: 200 pounds
(91 kilograms)

ARAPAIMA
Length: up to 15 feet
(4.6 meters)
Weight: up to 440 pounds
(200 kilograms)

Arapaimas have flat, greenish-gray heads. Their large mouths turn upward.

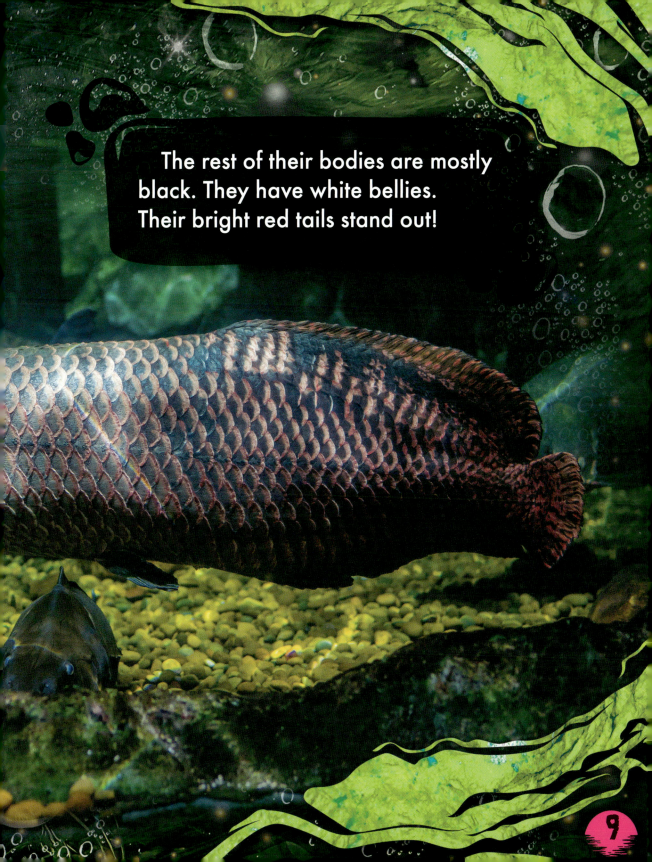

The rest of their bodies are mostly black. They have white bellies. Their bright red tails stand out!

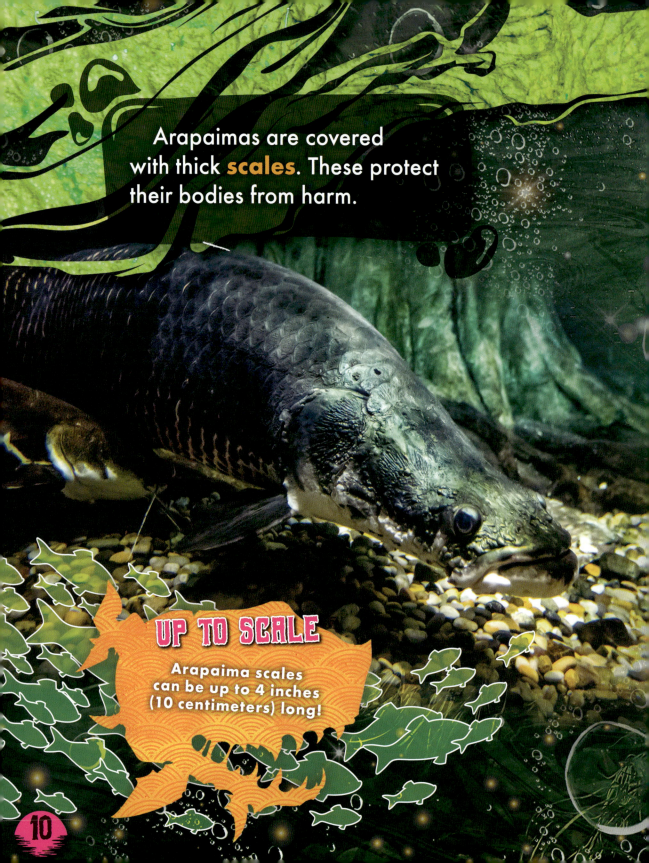

Arapaimas are covered with thick **scales**. These protect their bodies from harm.

UP TO SCALE

Arapaima scales can be up to 4 inches (10 centimeters) long!

IDENTIFY AN ARAPAIMA

FLAT HEAD **BIG MOUTH** **THICK SCALES** **SHARP TEETH**

They have bony tongues and many sharp teeth. They even have teeth on the roofs of their big mouths! These help arapaimas crush **prey**.

FINDING FOOD

Arapaimas swim slowly near the water's surface. They open their large mouths to suck up prey. Then they tear their food apart with their teeth and tongues.

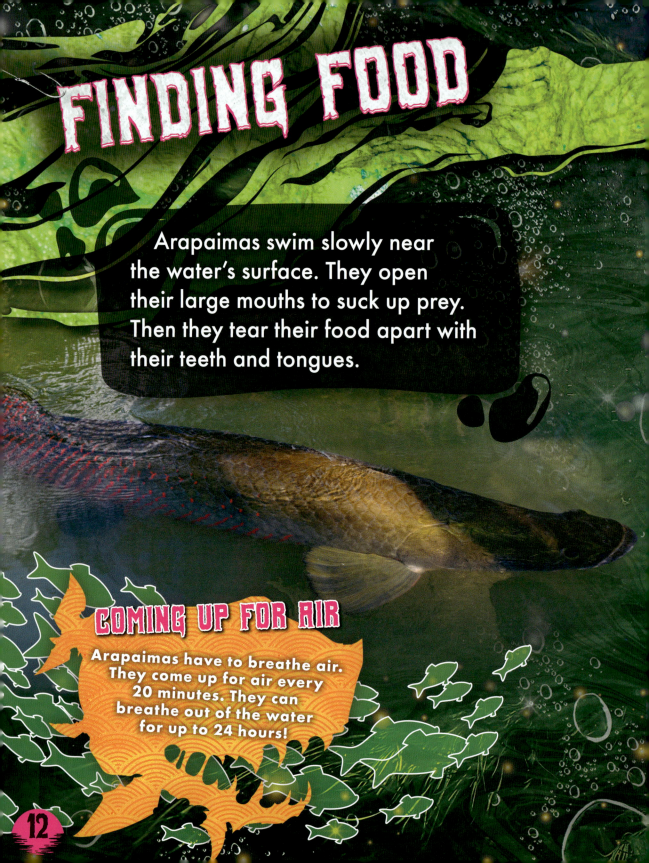

COMING UP FOR AIR

Arapaimas have to breathe air. They come up for air every 20 minutes. They can breathe out of the water for up to 24 hours!

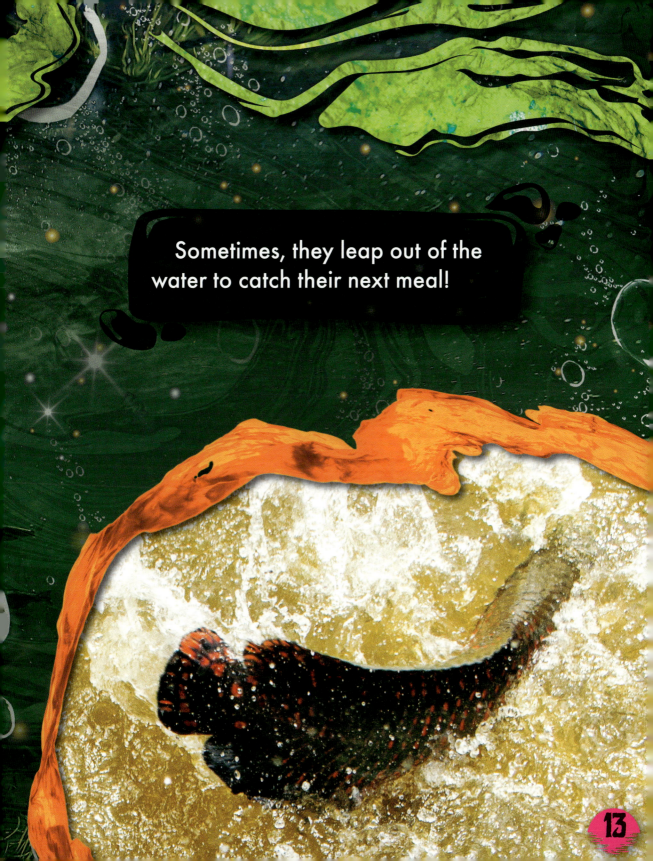

Sometimes, they leap out of the water to catch their next meal!

Arapaimas mostly eat fish and crabs. Even larger fish, such as piranhas, are no match for these deadly predators.

They eat other foods, too. They may eat fruits, seeds, and **insects**. They also eat birds and small **mammals**.

When arapaimas **spawn**, they build nests deep in the sand. Females lay thousands of eggs.

Both parents guard their eggs and **fry**. Males may hide fry in their mouths to protect them!

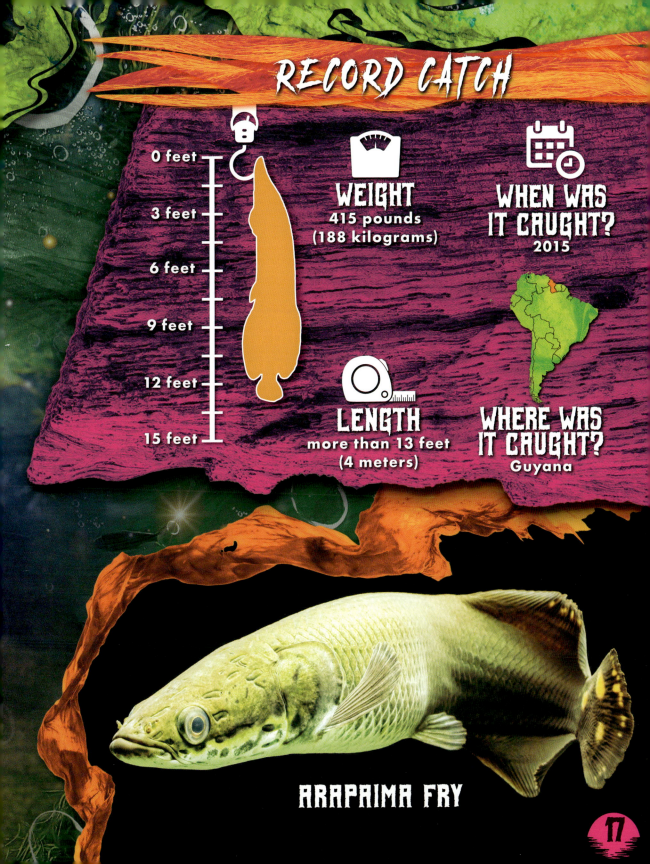

ARAPAIMAS IN TROUBLE

People like to buy and eat arapaimas. This makes them worth a lot of money. Fishers and **poachers** catch them. This has led to **overfishing**.

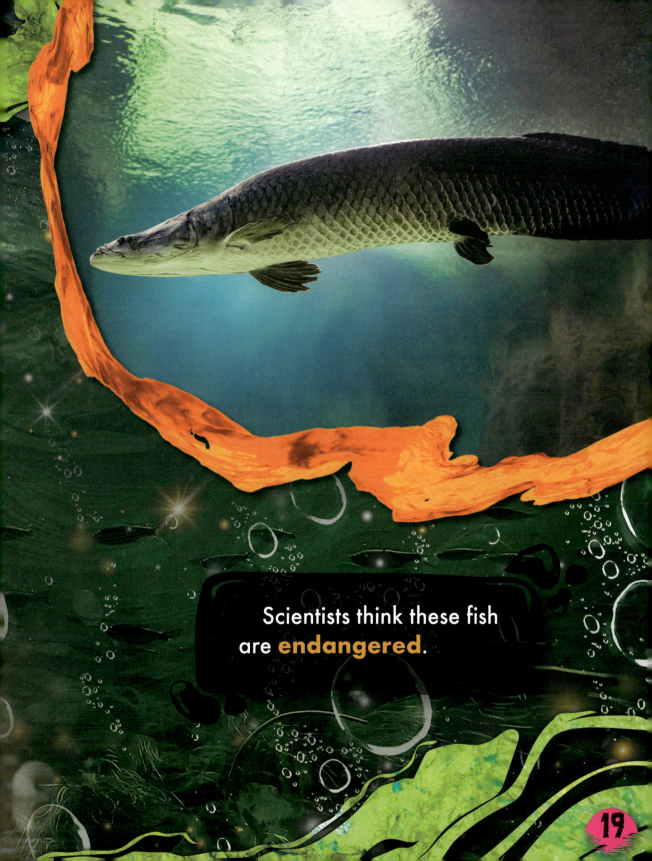

Scientists think these fish are **endangered**.

Local fishers are working to stop overfishing. They limit how many arapaimas they catch. They only catch these fish during certain times of the year. They look out for poachers.

This work will help arapaimas stay alive!

ARAPAIMA STATS

| LEAST CONCERN | NEAR THREATENED | VULNERABLE | ENDANGERED | CRITICALLY ENDANGERED | EXTINCT IN THE WILD | EXTINCT |

LIFE SPAN
up to 20 years

THREATS
overfishing, poaching

GLOSSARY

endangered—in danger of dying out

freshwater—related to water that is not salty

fry—young fish

insects—small animals with six legs and hard outer bodies; an insect's body is divided into three parts.

mammals—warm-blooded animals that have backbones and feed their young milk

overfishing—using up the number of fish by fishing too much

poachers—people who hunt animals illegally

predators—animals that hunt other animals for food

prey—animals that are hunted by other animals for food

rain forest—a thick, green forest that receives a lot of rain

scales—small plates that cover the bodies of some fish

spawn—to lay eggs

TO LEARN MORE

AT THE LIBRARY

Davidson, Rose. *Amazon Animals*. Washington, D.C.: National Geographic Kids, 2023.

Forest, Christopher. *Fish*. Minneapolis, Minn.: Abdo Publishing, 2021.

Lawrence, Ellen. *Arapaima*. New York, N.Y.: Bearport Publishing, 2017.

ON THE WEB

Factsurfer.com gives you a safe, fun way to find more information.

1. Go to www.factsurfer.com.

2. Enter "arapaimas" into the search box and click 🔍.

3. Select your book cover to see a list of related content.

INDEX

air, 12
Amazon Rain Forest, 4
bodies, 9, 10
colors, 8, 9
eggs, 16
endangered, 19
females, 16
fishers, 18, 20
food, 12, 13, 14, 15
fry, 16, 17
heads, 8
identify, 11
leap, 13
males, 16
mouths, 8, 11, 12, 16
name, 5
nests, 16
overfishing, 18, 20
people, 5, 18
poachers, 18, 20
predators, 4, 14
prey, 11, 12
range, 4, 5
record catch, 17
scales, 10
size, 6, 7, 10
South America, 4
spawn, 16
stats, 21
tails, 9
teeth, 11, 12
tongues, 11, 12

The images in this book are reproduced through the courtesy of: SergioRocha, cover (hero); Rocksweeper, pp. 2-3, 22-23, 24 (background); mokjc, p. 4; N-sky, pp. 6-7; panida wijitpanya, p. 8; Chalit Silpsakulsuk, pp. 8-9; kapulya, p. 10; Krivitskaya, p. 11 (flat head); Mikhail Mironov, p. 11 (big mouth); SakdatornSong, p. 11 (thick scales); Anna Aostojska, p. 11 (sharp teeth); TatianaMironenko, p. 11; Anton_AV, p. 12; MTur Destinos/ Wiki Commons, p. 13; Natnan Srisuwan, p. 14; Photoshot, pp. 14-15; ARCO/K. Hinze, pp. 16-17; Jorge Saenz/ AP Newsroom, p. 18; ivSky, p. 19; Pulsar Imagens/ Alamy, pp. 20-21; Amazon-Images MBSI/ Alamy, p. 21.